the l.h. octaves emulate the r.h. slurs in the rondo-theme.

The form is a sonata-rondo with a monothematic absorption in its opening figure. In the middle episode, b.143, a musette-like idea provides a temporary haven in A major, best played close to the keys and with lightness and simplicity but yielding just a touch of pathos with the minor-key inflections in bb.161–165. The leads into b.143 and b.175 need no *ritardando* beyond a slight 'placing' to mark the surprise of the major and the return of the minor. The closing section increases in intensity, and the shock of bb.199–202 is carried through in sustained *f*. A keen orchestral sense is called for in the last three lines. Reducing the 'scoring' to a pair of oboes in bb.233–236 will underline the abrupt contrast of dynamics. This passage may be divided between the hands, in which case the r.h. fingering should replace *5454*, etc., with *4343*. Short slurs may be implied here in the manner of the rondo-theme. Note that the canon in bb.245–250 includes the repeated octave Es, and treat the final chords with orchestral precision.

D.M.

GW00499605

TEXTUAL NOT

Composition   Paris, summer 1778

Sources   autograph, in New York private collection (formerly in the Preussische Staatsbibliothek, Berlin) [A]; first edition, as no.2 of *Trois sonates pour le clavecin ou le forte piano . . . Oeuvre IV* (Paris: Heina, 1782) [E]

Notes   The text basically follows A; where E is the source of an emendation or a possible alternative reading this is noted below, but faults in E, which is inaccurate, are noted only when of possible significance

1st movt
A: LH notated in tenor clef, 1–5 (1st beat), 9–14 (1st beat); in alto clef, 50–6, 104–5

bar

3	A lacks slur
6	E has *f* (no *p* in LH, or *f* in 9)
7	staccato marks in E
9	as 3
10	LH top note *e'* in E (also originally in A, but altered)
22	LH bottom note *B'* in E
45	*f* editorial: Mozart gave no dynamic marks in A after 23 but it is inconceivable that *forte* should not be reached by this point, if not sooner; E gives *f* at 49
46	E has *f* in middle of bar, but this is a misreading of Mozart's clarifying instruction 'si' next to the smudged note *b'* in A
50–6	LH all 8ve lower in E as in all passages which in A are in alto clef in this sonata (except 104–5 in this movement, 167–74 in 3rd movement); this seems certain to be an error

76–7	notated as 'bis' from 74–5; presumably LH *E–e* chord not intended in 76 (though thus in E)
80–7	not written out; Mozart's instruction 'Da capo 8 mesures'; *d♯"* acciaccatura omitted as clearly redundant (though thus in E)
92	RH, 2nd half of bar, lower note *e'* in A, *f'* (correctly) in E; LH, last slur in E only
126	*f* editorial; cf. 45 above; E gives *f* at 133

2nd movt
A: LH notated in alto clef, 6 (3rd crotchet)–7, 15 (2nd)–19 (1st), 28 (3rd)–30 (1st), 36 (2nd and 3rd), 66 (3rd)–67 (1st, 1st note of 2nd), 70 (2nd note)–72 (1st note): all these passages notated an 8ve lower in E

bar

4	Mozart's slurring ambiguous; it seems to read:

5	RH hard to decipher, probably on 2nd and 3rd crotchets; any correction involves guesswork (ours preserves the 2nd repeated *c"*, which also appears in E: 1st time, as A in 59)
20	RH stacc. only in E
27	*p* here exactly as placed by Mozart; possibly it should be at *9* or *17*
44–9	A, original notation: etc
54–60	not written out; Mozart's instruction 'Da capo 7 mesures'
81	A: RH *p* halfway through bar; but cf. 26
82	analogous to 27

3rd movt
bar

1–20	LH slurring left exactly as Mozart wrote it, despite apparent inconsistency, as its presence or absence has definite harmonic significance (also 107–21, 175–93)
8	possibly LH chord *e–e'* intended on 1st beat, but it seems that Mozart originally wrote, then eliminated, the *e* (which is retained in E)
91–4	LH, 1 slur per bar (except 92), but cf. 87–90
107	see 1–20
159–60	RH, 1 slur per bar (at end/beginning of staff)
167	LH in alto clef to 174, *1*
173	RH upper notes *b'*, *c"*, *d"* (crotchet, 2 qs) in A; E as shown
175	see 1–20
226–9	RH slurred only 227, 229, 1 slur per bar; cf. LH and 56–9

Editorial notes
In the printing of the text a distinction has been made between original and editorial markings. Slurs and ties added editorially are indicated by a small perpendicular stroke; editorial staccato marks (whether dots or wedges), dynamic markings and accidentals are indicated by the use of smaller type.

SONATA in A minor

K310/300d (1778)

© 1981 by The Associated Board of the Royal Schools of Music

10

12

Andante cantabile

* The rhythmic pattern shown for bar 20 may be preferred here and in parallel contexts (e.g. bars 24, 25).

A.B.1691

Presto

21

A.B.1691

22

Printed in England by Caligraving Limited Thetford Norfolk

**The Associated Board of
the Royal Schools of Music
(Publishing) Limited**

14 Bedford Square
London WC1B 3JG

ISBN 1-85472-172-0

9 781854 721723